Bring a Torch, Jeannette, Isabella

Tuba

traditional French carol
arranged by Luther Henderson

T0039508

Ding Dong! Merrily On High

Tuba

traditional carol
arranged by Luther Henderson

Go Tell It On The Mountain

Tuba

19th century Negro Spiritual
arranged by Luther Henderson

God Rest Ye Merry Gentlemen

Tuba

traditional London carol, 19th century tune
arranged by Luther Henderson

Here We Come A-Wassailing

Tuba

traditional carol from the north of England
arranged by Luther Henderson

The Huron Carol

Tuba

traditional carol
arranged by Luther Henderson

I Saw Three Ships

traditional English carol
arranged by Luther Henderson

Tuba

Sussex Carol

Tuba

traditional English carol
arranged by Luther Henderson